Vitals

Narin S. Kilic

Vitals

Copyright © 2024 by Narin S. Kilic.
Illustrations rendered by:
Narin S. Kilic

All rights reserved. No part of this publication may be reproduced, distributed, or transmitted in any form or by any means, including photocopying, recording, or other electronic or mechanical methods, without the written consent of the publisher. The only exceptions are for brief quotations included in critical reviews and other non-commercial uses permitted by copyright law.

MILTON & HUGO L.L.C.
4407 Park Ave., Suite 5
Union City, NJ 07087, USA

Website: *www.miltonandhugo.com*
Hotline: *1-888-778-0033*
Email: *info@miltonandhugo.com*

Ordering Information:
Quantity sales. Special discounts are granted to corporations, associations, and other organizations. For more information on these discounts, please reach out to the publisher using the contact information provided above.

Library of Congress Control Number: 2024919574
ISBN-13:   979-8-89285-266-1 [Paperback Edition]
                  979-8-89285-267-8 [Hardback Edition]
                  979-8-89285-265-4 [Digital Edition]

Rev. date: 08/20/2024

This book is dedicated to my family and those who I consider it.

Common things are hard to spot,
unless you've done your research on my burnt-out soul.
-naive

Table of Contents

Chapter I	The Brain	1
Chapter II	The Heart	31
Chapter III	The Lungs	55
Chapter IV	Blood	73
Chapter V	Pulse	97
Chapter VI	Flatline	119
Chapter VII	Solemn words	151

The Brain

The brain is the biggest and most complex organ within our meaningless bodies. More than 100 billion nerves come together to allow you to feel and think. It is the command center. The leader of the group. More or less something that's actually important.

Your brain will do whatever it yearns to do to you. Wanna be sad? Your brains got you. Wanna freak out over something that's only 200 calories? Cool now you have an eating disorder. Did you only take one hit off that vape?
Welcome to a nicotine addiction.

Some days it will really feel like your whole ass brain fell out of your head. At that point you may feel a haze that seems never ending...

One day we'll all escape the road of disaster our brains put us on, but now we're stuck with coping in our own unhealthy ways.

Vitals

My head feels like it's taking a drive on the never ending highway hidden in the clouds
-dissociation

Vitals

Welcomed with open and loving arms,
Not to notice the growing **shadow** cast upon our souls.
For theirs to only turn to anger and disgust towards the one they had originally welcomed so dearly in the beginning, But how quickly they had seemed to brush off and continue their growing **evil** in their own souls just to torture another's
-crusades and agitation

Vitals

Death to all who said I made a mistake.

I don't need to be told what I already know.
-carnage

Vitals

When the dial drops I can finally tell myself that I've won,

But at what cost?

You won't see me as beautiful anyways.
-cursed

Vitals

She *vanished,*
And took every remaining hope I had along with her on a string of regrets and chances
-calamity

Vitals

If a picture is worth a thousand words...
What did *mine* tell you?
-*camera*

Vitals

I guess the singed parts of my fucking heart and the swimming pools of tears never were enough for you asshole's
-controversy, altercation, rage, and death

Vitals

How uplifting must it feel to end up in someone's sob story bullshit poems?
Now that you know that you actually did get under my skin.
-*catastrophe*

Vitals

Are you
d i s h e a r t e n e d
because I'm back now?
-rage

Vitals

My wishes,
To take back the control of the wheel,
To be thinner,
To be smaller,
To be...

gone.
-change

Vitals

Losing the grip that was once strong,
But has grown weak,
The grip finally let go,
And the eyes of many meet fate.
-falling

Vitals

I let the walls that were so strong and slammed shut to be cracked open just a bit,
Only to find out they had been made of sand, and not as strong as everyone thought they once were.
-*zero*

Vitals

I was done with everything for so long.
You finally gave me a rightful excuse to pick up my shit and go.
I hope you're happier when I'm gone
Because hearing your voice and being in *your* presence..
Makes me sick.

-zoophagous

The Heart

The heart is the muscular vessel that pumps blood throughout your entire body. It sends blood towards your brain encouraging the spiraling thoughts that take over your emotions and the things you do. The heart brings pain when loved ones go, and sorrow when they never return.

Sometimes you let your heart take control… when all you really needed to do was let go. Your heart does some crazy shit.

In all honesty I'm sure we can all agree that the heart isn't that necessary. Like what are you gonna do without it? Die? Who gives a shit? Not me. Like, you will 110% not make it without a heart, but if it already brings you so much pain as it is, what is death gonna bring you? Nothing you didn't already want.

If you go through heartbreak it feels like your heart is going to burst. Just full on get up and fucking explode. So what? Last time I checked my heart is still here after a horrible heartbreak, and I'm kinda mad about it. Hopefully one day it actually does explode.

Vitals

I want to be able to hear your name without having a sharp unbearable pain in my chest,
But you won't let that happen.
Will you?
-construction

Vitals

Falling on,
Falling on you,
Falling in,
Falling in love,
Falling in lust,
Falling in sin,
Falling on end,
Falling in failure,
Falling in darkness,
Falling back,
Going back,
Not wanting to go back,

help.
-falling in…

Vitals

You,
You have torn me apart.
Limb by limb,
Nerve by nerve,
Taking whatever left you can find,
And **burning** it in the flames of your actions and words,
All at fucking once.
-for no one

I,
I am,
I am lost,
I am,
I am numb.
I,
I have,
I have lost control,
I have lost me.
I,
I need,
I need you to shut me off and make it **stop**.
I,
I need help.
-off

Vitals

I've never seen so much pain and happiness at the same time
 in the eyes of anyone else,
But you.
-*know*

Vitals

One truthfully explosive pair,
But when coming in contact with the naive,
Everything becomes catastrophic.
-blithe and kindness

Vitals

Those eyes could make your whole body shake with just once glance
-confusion

Vitals

I wish I never looked in that direction
-confusion .II

Vitals

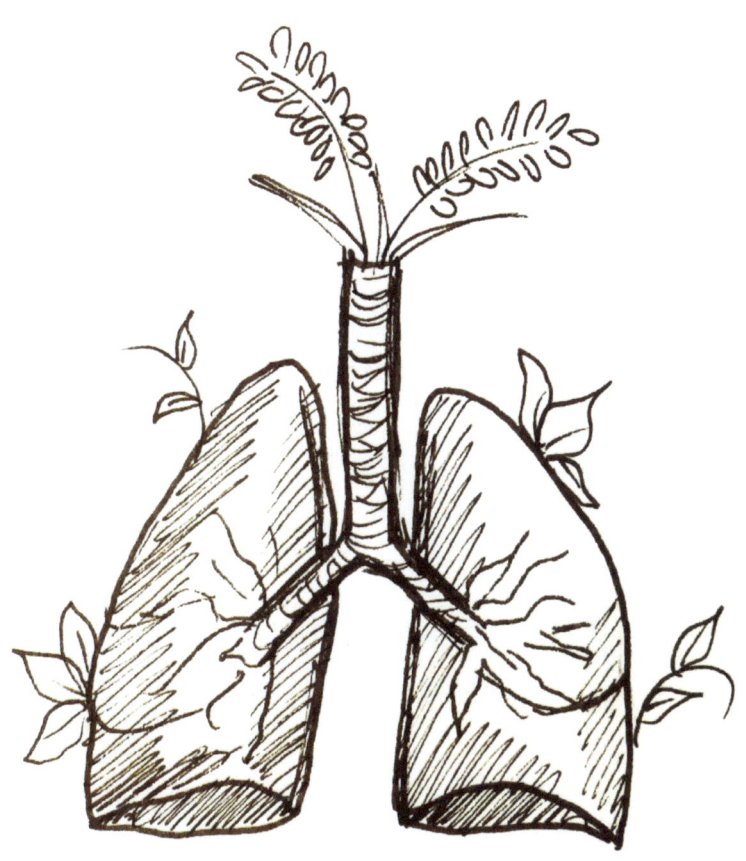

The Lungs

The lungs are spongy air sacs that lie on each side of the chest. Air is inhaled through them to bring in oxygen to keep you from dying.

It is the first thing you do the minute you escape the womb, and the last thing you do before you say goodbye to this desolate world.

Breathing can give you a sense of knowing that you are alive. To feel the air run in and out of your lungs at a quick pace gives some sort of fulfillment. When you decide to hold in those breaths to allow the feeling of light rush through your body… that is when you will really feel the most alive. It gives you the feeling that you have some control, even if it's a little bit, it is enough to make you feel alright when your kingdom is crumbling around you.

Maybe holding in that last breath is the best thing to do. Or maybe letting it out and never breathing back in is the way to go.

Take a moment now to relax…
Breathe in.

Breathe out.

Vitals

Oh, how I ache to tell you so many things
But oh, how I fear that you will no longer love me the way you do
And oh, how I fear not getting the chance to tell you those things
Because one day I might not get to.
-mother

Vitals

How I yearn for the embers of my own to flutter across the night sky,
So that I can finally

B
    R
        E
            A
                T
                    H
                        E

-nourishing

Vitals

I am so glad you are out of my life,
I wasn't happy with you anyways.
-goodbye

Vitals

I'd like to ask you once again,
If a picture is worth a thousand words..
What did mine tell you?
That you fucked up?
-*zany*

Vitals

Breathing.
-first mistake

Vitals

Thank you for giving me countless moments to
SCREAM.
For that, I am forever in your debt.
-breath

Vitals

There is an unholy amount of screaming that I have done,
And I don't plan for it to be over until I draw my last breath.
-aggrieve

Vitals

My numbness and pain will forever reside with each breath I take,
For however long it pleases.
-tourment

The only way I know how to feel full is if my stomach is not.
-*empty*

Vitals

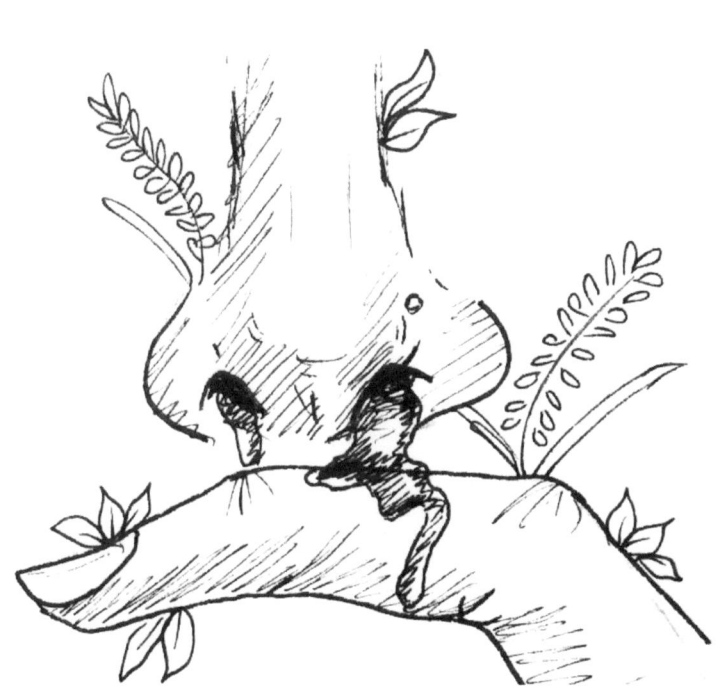

Blood

Blood is a thick red fluid that courses through your veins bringing oxygen and nutrients to the cells in your body. Without blood nothing in the body would work. Your body would be deprived of oxygen, thus resulting in death.

I get nose bleeds often . I feel a rush of wetness in my left nostril as blood trickles down my face for reasons I don't know, and probably will never know. Maybe it's just my body telling me that I am alive.

The sight of blood can make many feel weak. Why feel weak? Blood is there to make you live. I understand it though. To see something that keeps you alive outside of your body. That has to be it.

Vitals

When two become one,
I am no longer just me,
Then I find *you* and become we.
-we

Vitals

I never thought that I could be so happy for so long,
And yet,
So quickly torn into pieces.
By you.
-zealous

Goodbye. I will **never** miss you.
    -forget

Vitals

Someday I will be able to hear that song without crying out in pain.
Someday I will be able to see your face without immediately looking in the opposite direction.
Someday I will say hello, and you will acknowledge it and answer back.
Someday you will be able to say my name without an utter hatred in your voice.
Someday,
But not today.
-*soon*.

Words in the end are completely meaningless when they are taken and thought on.
-strength

Vitals

Never have,
Never will,
Well at least only to you,
But you don't believe me.
-lie

Vitals

There are none.
-truth

Vitals

Even at a young age, most boys never were able to give me that same warm hearted and happy feeling that *girls* do. Loving *girls* is one of the things that I know how to do better I guess.

- not much of a surprise

Vitals

Pure smiles and late nights were all I wanted,
But I guess you didn't.
Did you love?
-*cause*

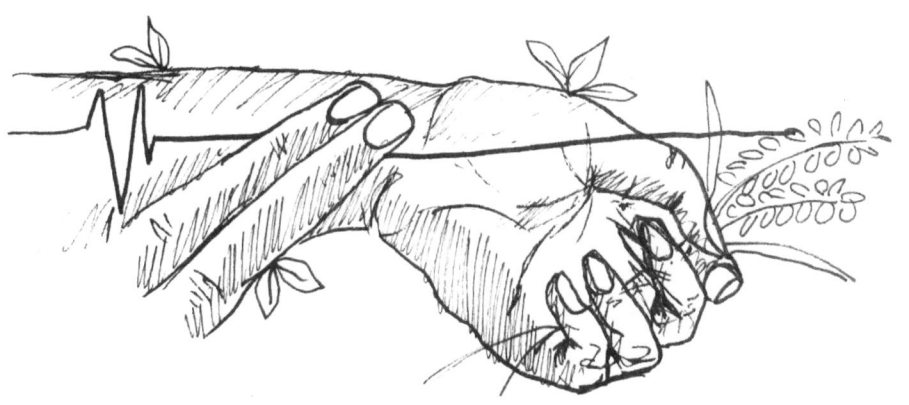

Pulse

Vitals

Alive. Your pulse is the only thing keeping you from leaving a world that only brings pain. Gym classes in high school teach you how to use your pulse to calculate your heart rate. You can find your pulse just about anywhere on your body. The beat of your heart resonates through every pump.

If you learn to live with the fact that your pulse could stop at any moment, are you really willing to live?

You could be having the time of your life and suddenly it's all taken away once the heart stops beating, and your pulse is nowhere to be found. Just like that. It's all over. Will you know it's even happening?

Honey is a tragedy to my ears.
How sad.
It was such a nice song,
- *calamity .11*

Vitals

A familiar face shines brighter bringing through the deeply
dug hole of her own
Pain
And
Regrets
-hello

Vitals

Asking is no longer itself when it is constant,
By then it becomes begging.
My begging for you
To stop
And just
Listen.
-don't

No one ever suspects the "pretty" girl.
-*suspicions*

Vitals

It's sad,
That I am so desperate to the point where I will throw away everything,
Just for one kiss.
-games

Vitals

I should've known from the minute I even questioned it….
-*curious*

Vitals

With every wave to crash down on a beach,
Another heart breaks with it.
-truth .II

Vitals

The relationship I have with food is equivalent to the events of exes trying to be friends
It just doesn't work out.
-calamity .II

YOU'RE A DIFFERENT WAVELENGTH AND I CAN'T GO IN YOU'RE A DIFFERENT WAVELENGTH AND I CAN'T GO IN YOU'RE A DIFFERENT WAVELENGTH AND I CAN'T GO IN YOU'RE A DIFFERENT WAVELENGTH AND I CAN'T GO IN YOU'RE A DIFFERENT WAVELENGTH AND I CAN'T GO IN

WHY IS EVERYTHING SO LOUD

The screams won't stop
I've turned to a different station
Thoughts echo into a piercing screech
The cars are crashing
Crashing
THEY'RE FUCKING CRASHING
JUST FUCKING STOP IT

It's all just ringing
Ringing
Ringing
Ringing
No no no no no no
NO MORE PLEASE
-secluded

Flatline

Death. The only promise at the end of a tragic story. The end of your story will always be determined by pixels in a line on a screen followed by a long beep after. No matter what accomplishments you may have made through your sorrow filled life, they all dissipate in the end. Completely meaningless.

So why does it matter? Why do we fight for a life that will end anyways? Maybe to find a sense of humanity. Maybe so that we feel like throughout our lives we could've possibly meant anything to the world. Or maybe not. Maybe people just live because they are scared of dying.

Are you?

I am. No matter how much in my life I talk about incoming death.. I will always be afraid.

Vitals

Hey,
Welcome back
Yeah
No not really
Why?
No. Stop.
Screaming isn't necessary.
Ok.
Maybe later.
I know.
I know. I know.
I'll talk to you later.
Yeah, I know you'll always be here
No matter how much I want you to go.
Bye for now.
-a dance on the beach

Vitals

Watch my face sink into the sands of time as my bones become alive and dance throughout this pretty night.
-mummy

Vitals

The groans don't bother me anymore,
I view them as a sign of success.
My wish is nearly fulfilled.
-the sleeping giant

From the remnants of a past fire,
A sense of agony rushes over the wounded area.
Bubbling up from what was once healthy skin,
Sat a huge annoyance,
That was only there to use and bother the occupying skin
Until it was done with the once thriving skin,
To blow up and never return again.
-*blister (continuation to breath)*

Vitals

I can hear you when I don't want to.
You can never hear me.
I've tried to call you.
You only scream out to the sea.
My ears are ringing.
It's time to give in.
To the things surrounding.
And the creatures in my skin.
-no two can play one game

When I take in the scent of your sharp pains,
I miss the days when I called you mine.
-alcohol

Vitals

It's been months since I've taken in your dwindling spell of warmth. The burning allowed for the pains on the inside to go away with each sip.
-alcohol .II

With the time spent chasing after an apparition in a dark forest,
I had yet to see the light shine through.
-realization

Vitals

I find that the feeling of a simple kiss to the forehead can bring the warmth back into my frostbitten body
-recreate

Vitals

The human senses decide on their own time for when it's ok to return from the barricaded walls along the castle.
Although, it's frightening when they are gone for too long.
-knight

Vitals

A face so strong and sharp that could make you feel scared and safe all at once.
With the knowledge that you are safe while there, and scared for the others who approach it.
-*radiant*

Vitals

Hopefully by the end of this bittersweet song the notes won't go sour..
-reluctant

"I'd like to see a happy book someday."
Happiness doesn't come without pain love.
-reimagine

Vitals

She wilts when the coldness of the winter swallows her
 spirits as the sky grows darker.
Until, the sun cuts through in the spring and allows her to
B R E A T H E
Once more.

-rose

Solemn Words

Vitals

Throughout my life I have learned many things.

Hating has become my specialty. There are grudges that run so deep through my soul that maybe I'll never be able to let them go. My grip of hatred against others will forever be the sole reason why I can't grow up. Although, growing up can happen to people so easily. Age is merely a drop of water in the large pond that is growing up. Being sheltered my whole life, only now am I just opening up the doors of the real world.. and I'm scared. It's terrifying to me when I've been shut in the doors of childhood for so long. I fear for my future. What is to become of me in my old age. Who will I be? Will I have a name for myself? Or will I whittle away as those who I once loved die off. Being left alone the way it all started. Alone. Alone with my thoughts late at night. The pain of wanting to be small. I fight with myself even now. A friend of mine passed away recently as I write this. What became of him. Only a memory of what once was. Someone who was destined for greatness. I never realized how close we were until I looked at the messages we shared over time. To have someone confide in me and trust me with their thoughts. I'd have to admit. He was an asshole. But I feel like he was covering up the way he really felt about things. I could see through it all, but I was never brave enough to release my thoughts into words. Now he's gone. His funeral card lies in my bag reminding me. Staring at me all the time. Death can come at any time. Did he expect it? None of us did. It hurts to be the one that knew everything leading up to his end. This weight lays on my chest heavy and hard. The one I currently love doesn't fully grasp the way everything went down. How will I die? Will it be quick? Will I even know it's happening? Do I want to die? Sometimes I ponder on what would happen if everything just suddenly stopped. Who would go to my funeral? Would anyone go? Stopping to think about this sinks my brain into the deepest part of the ocean. Lost. I've been lost for too long. My relationship with food is broken. From

the beginning of being told I have a small waist and the yearning to keep it that way to look appealing and beautiful. To restrict my want to eat after fights with my family to get back at them. I am not sure if I was really getting back at them, but the joke was really being played on myself. I liked the way the lack of food entering my body looked. The way I could better see my ribs through my porcelain skin. I've grown to enjoy hunger pains. The feeling of emptiness, but my need to keep going and moving all collided so well. What will become of me? Was it all worth it? This feeling I have, my jumble of words typed on paper. What is it all for? There are so many things I have locked away. Four years have passed since I started spilling my thoughts into this book. Four years. Yet, I am still here looking back into the words of a sad and used 15 year old. To feel this way at such a young age shouldn't have happened. This hurts. I hate the way I perceive the world around me. Growing up is scary. The world is empty. It's dark and solemn. I am trying. I am trying so fucking hard. God fuck. I don't understand any of this. Nothing makes sense in my head. My life is one spinning circle. I'm just waiting for this circle to end. But I'm learning. I'm watching. I'm healing. From the pains of the past and the present. It's going to take a long time. I am ready for it. I'm not. But I'll try. Learning that I am not truly alone. Learning to speak and not lock myself inside of my own head.
Learning how to truly be human.

Thank You.

The End.

Narin Kilic is a 22 year old college graduate. She had a bachelor's degree in Forensic Science. Cool right. She's not exactly sure what she is going to do with her life, but she knows that it will most likely work out in the end. She was born in New Jersey, but her parents moved her family to south Florida. Crazy shit happens everyday, it's Florida though so what did she expect? Life moves on as she tries to find her way through the deeply rooted vines of life. Only time will tell what will become of her greatness, but she hopes everything will go well.

Picture taken May 2021

◯ @notnarin

www.ingramcontent.com/pod-product-compliance
Lightning Source LLC
Chambersburg PA
CBHW041801160426
43191CB00001B/1